Six Lessons

with Delphi

How to Live Happily with All Life

by
Patricia Jepsen
and
Delphi

"A Happiness Book for All Ages"

Also by Patricia Jepsen (Chuse)

Delphi, What Being on Earth Is All About
The GodSelf, Revelation for the New Millennium
The Workbook, Study Guide for The GodSelf

Copyright © 2002 by Patricia Jepsen Chuse

Bright World Publishing
Patricia Jepsen Chuse
P.O. Box 913
Ojai, California 93024

e-mail: delphinet@mindspring.com

Illustrations by Kimberley Hevesy
Lyrics and music copyright © 2002
by Patricia Jepsen Chuse
Music notation by Naomi Stephan, Ph.D.
Cover design by Osiris Castañeda
Earth Treaty on page 15 designed by Emily Praetorius

Library of Congress Control Number: 2002108946
ISBN 0-9667560-2-9

Printed in the United States of America

*To the World of Animals
and to All
Who Love Them*

Table of Contents

Introduction

I wanted a golden retriever and Delphi (pronounced Delpheee) wanted to get out of the dog show business. We found each other at a kennel in Virginia.

I loved animals and I had already developed an ability to communicate with them. I thought that was fun. But, there was something different in the way Delphi communicated and expressed herself. She wasn't cute and doggy. She was precise and profound in the way she expressed herself, and she was very wise. It took a while for me to understand that Delphi wanted to be a teacher and that what she was looking for was not a mistress, not even a pal, but someone who could hear her and write down what she had to say.

It wasn't my idea to "teach" animal communication. The whole idea was Delphi's. She pointed out to me that we should team up and advertise that we were in the animal communication business. I must say I was a bit hesitant because, although I could understand animals and they could understand me—which had resulted in some small miracles between "owner" and "pet"—I had absolutely no experience, had attended no animal communication workshops and had no idea how I communicated. Still...somehow...Delphi encouraged me to just *advertise*. Well, we did, and we have been teaching and coaching communication with all life ever since!

Delphi and my other two golden retriever partners, Chipper and Light, have guided me into a world of wonder, so much love and incredible wisdom. They have introduced me to amazing children who truly believe that dogs can speak, and they have uncompromisingly showed me the child in the heart.

How did this all happen? Why did Delphi and I write *Six Lessons with Delphi?* I had just completed a book entitled *Delphi, What Being on Earth Is All About* that told the story of my life with Delphi. Soon after the book was finished, I began to receive requests to write a study course on animal communication. So, I got together with Delphi to discuss the matter. She loved the idea and went right to work dictating to me her wisdom teachings.

Soon after spiral binding the lessons and passing them out to several of Delphi's favorite students, orders began to come in. Schools, community organizations, churches, and the women's unit of Wilmot Prison in Tucson, Arizona, were among the *Six Lessons'* customers. As I write this, over 2,500 spiral-bound copies have been sold. All copied, collated and bound in my small office with the help of Delphi volunteers! And the call for *Six Lessons with Delphi* is continuing as I write this.

Letters began coming in, addressed to Delphi. Heartwarming and heartbreaking letters from "children" of all ages who wrote that *Six Lessons* had changed their lives. It was following the first group of letters from the women's prison that I knew that *Six Lessons with Delphi* had a life of its own. People of every age and culture were responding to a little, home-published, "just for fun" book written by a golden retriever.

Do I really hear or sense Delphi speaking? Yes. But then, so many people have confided in me over the last few years that they, too, know that their dog or cat is speaking. We can all understand nature and our animal partners; perhaps not exactly as I do, but we can communicate and we can realize a living partnership with our planet and all life upon this planet.

In the communication classes that Delphi and I have hosted, I have seen genuine healing, both psychological and physical. And what we have experienced in these classes has been a deeper understanding of relationships, a depth of communication and a gentler way of living. Now, with *Six Lessons with Delphi,* the gift of a New World can be shared—a world where everyone is related from dolphin to porcupine, little child to tree. We are all one happy family on earth, or so Delphi says.

We have forgotten our place in the circle of life, Delphi tells us; it is time to return to community partnership where we all work together as a team. Community means all life. When we feel companionship with all life, emptiness is filled; we feel connected and loved.

As I review my companionship with Delphi and the ways that she acts and reacts with me, I sense she is a very special spark who lights my world and the world of those who respond to her presence and her lessons.

These lessons are for the whole family, to be read and discussed together. They are for the quiet reading corner, hidden from the world, where the magic of Delphi can be remembered and understood.

An eleven-year-old friend and student of Delphi remarked that her deepest wish after reading the Harry Potter books was to receive an invitation to the Wizard School. That invitation didn't come, though she waited and waited. But then, she met Delphi and was invited to join the Delphi School! In the Wizard School, she pointed out, you use a wand to perform magic. But in the Delphi School, you use your heart. "It's Heart Magic," she said. Delphi was listening, and when the young person had finished speaking, Delphi looked genuinely pleased. "That's Proper Magic," Delphi said. And they both laughed and agreed it was!

Patricia Jepsen

Meet Delphi

My name is Delphi and I would like you to be a partner with me. I am a golden retriever by birth.

I came to this planet to help everybody. I saw that Mother Earth needed help and so I came—as did other persons like myself. We are more like angels than what you call animals. This is because we know a lot. And we carry a lot of love with us. Bundles of love, in fact. I hope you can feel my love when I write this, because I really want you to. I want you to love just like I do. That's what these lessons are about...loving one another like brothers and sisters and taking good care of Mother Earth.

Perhaps it is new to you that dogs can speak. That is my mission...to let you know that. There are some books out now by very smart people that do tell you about this. Of course, all life is speaking. You do know that, don't you? We have to listen, that's all. Most of us don't listen. We have to learn to listen and to believe. I think lots of little kids have understanding about this already...and then some of them forget when they go to school to learn things like arithmetic and reading!

So, I am writing this book with my partner, Pat. Pat and I are almost one person when we write. Of like mind, so to speak. If you will now begin Lesson One, believing that I am speaking, you will learn a lot. I hope so, anyway!

Your friend,

Delphi

Lesson One
The Earth Has a Body

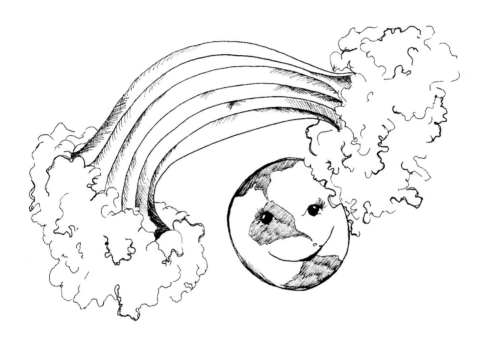

We are all united in one body
that is called Earth.
That is why we have to take care of her.

Delphi

Hi! My name is Delphi...

Hi! My name is Delphi...

and I know a lot about Mother Earth and all the animals on the Earth.

Mother Earth feels trapped now because people haven't taken care of her properly. She is very sad. I know, because she told me so. Please help her, she needs your help.

Here is my picture so that you will know who I am. You can learn more about me by checking out my web site: www.delphinet.org.

Well, let's get back to Mother Earth because that's what I really want to talk about—how you can help her to feel happy.

The Circle of Life

Everyone is related. I mean EVERYONE. That is the way we were made...like cousins, uncles, sisters and brothers. I like to think of everyone as family. I'll give you an example of what I am talking about.

Pretend you are seeing one of the dog people in front of you. (I call them "people," you may not. But that's okay too.)

Let's pretend you see a dog person and you say, instead of "dog," UNCLE DOG. See what I mean? That denotes respect. Or SISTER HORSE. Of course, when you know their true name—like mine is Delphi—then you can say SISTER DELPHI. How does that sound to you? That's the way you can begin to remember that we are really a CIRCLE OF LIFE, all connected together by Grandmother Love. Then no one will hurt another. We will all get along fine.

Okay...

You have learned a lot already, haven't you?

Do you have a notebook?

I think you need one with these lessons.

Then you can write down what you have learned.

You can make numbers in front of the LEARNING POINTS. They will stand out for you when you read them again.

The Real Laws

You know that in the beginning when the Creator made this Earth and all the people on her, the Creator also made real laws that we all knew and obeyed. There was nothing to hurt Earth at that time. We all knew each other as friends and helpers, and we all knew the REAL LAWS and lived peacefully by them. Then people forgot these laws and Earth was sad.

Too many trees began to be chopped down without asking. Most of the humans forgot that we all have voices to hear, hearts to know. Soon Earth was out of balance; weather forgot its duty to be kind to everyone. Most humans became separated in mind and heart from their brothers and sisters on Earth. Then it was that Mother Earth felt alone. She was very sad.

Many children are ready to help Mother Earth. But they don't know each other. That's the trouble. My plan is to connect all the children in the world together so that they can teach the grown-ups the REAL LAWS and how we should behave on our planet. If you are a grown-up already and would like to be a child again, then you can join my plan. We all are children in the heart! I know this for a fact!

The REAL LAWS have always been with us. The Creator made them so all could live in harmony and be happy. I would like to remind you of a few of them and then maybe you could tell me some...to add to the list.

Now, the Creator had this idea that Mother Earth was a person just like I am a person and you are a person. Mother Earth, as our planet, belongs in our hearts and minds. She is really our closest friend when it comes down to it. So, what I am saying here is RESPECT MOTHER EARTH. She has to be included in all our thoughts and actions. The words that we speak have to remember Mother Earth. Every step we take is WITH HER. The Creator laid down these laws about her so we would make a fine team in the solar system.

A solar system is a gathering of planets, stars, moons and a sun. They all get along together as one body under the Creator's real laws and His smile.

I know you have some thoughts of your own. I wouldn't mind hearing from you about this.

Write me a letter or send an e-mail to:
delphinet@mindspring.com.

IMPORTANT!

Here is a list of the REAL LAWS so you can remember them:

1. Always ask permission before you intrude into a person's place. Like...I wouldn't just come into your house without asking you, would I? Well, that's what I mean. So...RESPECT EVERYONE'S HOUSE is the first real law.

2. Don't hurt any of the people. (By people, I mean everyone.) To live in peace, we all have to care for one another. Imagine what it would be like on Mother Earth if we all obeyed that law!

3. A tree is a person too. You have to ask permission of a tree before you cut it down or even take one of its branches. When you break a branch off a tree suddenly, without asking permission first, it causes the tree pain. But when you ask permission first and the tree person says "yes," the tree does not suffer. But that's only if the tree says "yes," mind you! So I'm saying here: ASK PERMISSION BEFORE YOU TAKE ANYTHING. Don't just grab it! It's not yours until it gives itself to you. That's a law!

4. Thank the tree. If you will always say "thank you" when the tree gives you its branch, or the rain begins to fall, then there will be no shortage for anyone. Every "thank you" produces of itself a hundred times more abundance. PRACTICE SAYING "THANK YOU" FOR EVERYTHING. I think this is one of the most important of the real laws. I give thanks all of the time and I hope you do too! I always tell myself, "Delphi, if you don't give thanks, how will the Creator know where you are?"

5. Always remember that we are a family and we have to consider each one of us as special. I'm special, you're special. That way no one gets hurt. We are all happy together. And that's important! We will live in harmony and in peace if you do this. I WANT YOU TO KNOW THAT WE ARE ALL MEMBERS OF THE FAMILY OF EARTH AND WE ARE ALL RELATED.

The REAL LAWS are very important and need to be understood and then PRACTICED. Every law is important, remember that.

My Pink Ribbon Project and How You Can Join It

I have a special project that I call the PINK RIBBON PROJECT. This project is all about remembering that we are partners in the Circle of Life and that we have a job to do—each one of us—in this Circle.

What's your job? Write it in your notebook if you know it. You don't want to forget why you are here, you know!

Remember that I said that we are all bound together as a family with Mother Earth? Well, that's true enough. But I have more to say about this. The ribbon that binds us all together as one family is a bright pink. Just like I told you—the Pink Ribbon Project!

Pink is the color of love, and it is always love that connects us all together as the Circle of Life!

So, when you become a member of my Pink Ribbon Project, you are agreeing with Mother Earth and the Creator that we are all one family—human and animal. EVERYBODY! Each one of us is a person and each one of us is important. Every one of us has a job to do for Mother Earth. I know you know this but I am reminding you, just like I am reminding myself. Wear a pink ribbon now.

When you join my project, you can wear a bright pink ribbon. That ribbon means that you are an important member of the Circle of Life, that you practice the real laws and that you are a friend of Mother Earth.

Let me know what you think about all of this. I hope to hear from you soon.

Your Earth Treaty

*You can make a difference.
Mother Earth needs your help.
She is counting on you to
tell people how much she
needs their help too.*

I would like to tell you about the Earth Treaty Project because this is one way we can all help to make the earth better and a happier place to be. When you make a treaty, it is like a promise, you know. You can't go back on it.

Tell Mother Earth that you are going to help and then read your treaty to her. She might have some suggestions to make.

And send me a copy. I would like to know what you wrote too!

You can see what other kids have written on the next two pages. I think if you will write from your heart, it will be a very special treaty and will make Mother Earth smile.

Earth Treaty

You can make a difference

by Jill

The Earth was here for us... Let's be here for her.

MY EARTH TREATY

Mother Earth, I promise to make our planet better.

I will use scrap paper.

I won't waste any water.

I will help recycle cans and papers.

by Maureen

Lots of Homework...

1. Practice thinking that animals and plants and you and I are FAMILY. We are all part of the Circle of Life and we love one another.

2. After reading about the REAL LAWS, what other laws can you think of that would help Mother Earth and all the animals, plants and trees? Make a list of all the laws you can think of. And don't forget, I'd like to see them too!

3. Have you thought of your job to help Mother Earth? My job is to let people know that dogs can speak. Please wear a bright pink ribbon if you can think of your job.

And have a happy day!

Your friend,

Delphi

Lesson Two
Delphi's House

*Have you ever thought or even imagined
that you might be in the company of angels?*

*Delphi knows a lot about angels
and she would like to introduce you to them.*

*Come on into Delphi's house
and she will tell you about them!*

*There are important lessons here about the earth
community. I hope you will enjoy them.*

An Important Message
That You Can't Find Anywhere Else

This is what I have to say to you about my friends the angels and the nature spirits. They are perfect people, you know. You don't meet many perfect people, so this is a chance for you to really get to know perfect people and learn from them.

I wish you could see them the way I do. They are so nice looking. They can't frown. They don't even know how to frown. I think that is a good point to make. PERFECT PEOPLE DON'T FROWN. They have happy looks and laugh a lot. That's why they are called perfect. When you know how to smile all of the time, you will be like the angels.

There are not enough people smiling. I can tell you that right now. That's why Mother Earth needs you to smile. Smiles and laughter make people happy. And everyone needs happiness, I can tell you that! There are too many sad people. I bet you have sad people who frown a lot in your town. Write me about this. I want to know. After this lesson you will know how important it is to smile.

Your friend and special teacher,

Delphi

More Smiling!

Let's talk about smiling for awhile. Keep this in mind, one smile is worth a lot of frowns. There is no price on a smile! I can't think of a better gift to give anybody than your smile. Can you remember how many times you have smiled today?

I guess that is really hard to remember—how many times you have smiled. Do me a favor, will you? Carry a small notebook—the kind that fits in your pocket—and for the next three days, EVERY TIME YOU SMILE MAKE A MARK IN YOUR NOTEBOOK. That's right, keep a record of your smiles.

Maybe we could have a contest later on to see who can smile the most. That would be fun, wouldn't it?

No, I haven't forgotten about the angels. I really want to tell you about them...but smiling has to come first. You have to smile to meet an angel.

Are you ready to learn more? Good!

The Purpose of the Smile

Your smile is important. It adds to Mother Earth's happiness. She needs your smile to be happy herself. That's why my picture is in this book—to remind you to smile!

The reason the Creator gave us a smile is so we can be like the Sun. Did you know that the Sun shining is the Creator smiling at you? If you think this way you can't help but smile. I promise you that.

Now, first of all, you are probably saying, "Delphi, how come you are so smart about smiling? You can't smile. You're a dog. And positively dogs don't smile."

All right—fair enough. Here is a picture of me.

Do you see what I mean? I'm smiling.

All dogs smile, even the sad ones smile sometimes. They know the truth about smiling. Just as you do now.

What have you learned about smiling?

Write your answer in your notebook so that you will never forget it.

Be a Sun and Smile.

Everything that grows needs your smile. I think you know this but I'm telling you again.

One of the nicest things that you can do for yourself is to buy some sun stickers. Lots of stores carry them. You will find that they come in very handy!

Keep smiling!

Angels, Nature Spirits and Dogs

I think maybe dogs know angels better than anyone else. That is because we do the same work. Even though people don't know this yet, it's the truth.

Dogs and angels have a lot in common. They both carry a lot of love. I think babies have as many angels as we dogs do. That's because babies are fresh and new and they have a lot of knowledge that often gets forgotten when they grow up.

Let me explain about the nature spirits. Sometimes they are called "little people." They are very special. But most people haven't a clue as to who they are and what they do. On special days and in different times of the year, Native American peoples have ceremonies to thank the Creator and to appreciate Mother Earth. Often the "little people" are invited into the ceremonies.

I tell you now that these nature spirits are wonderful. You can feel them as GOOD ENERGY. That is what they are—Good Energy. You can call them that if you like. They make the rain to fall and the corn to grow and the breezes to cool your day. They are part of everything and we don't even know them! We have to understand this GOOD ENERGY is very important to our well-being as a planet and as a family.

There are groups of nature spirits and these groups have names like fairies, gnomes, undines, salamanders and sylphs. Everyone knows about fairies, but do you know what they do and why they are important to Mother Earth and all her family?

Fairies are people just like you and I—little people. They make things grow. They help people to laugh. They work with the angels to heal and to bring happiness to everything that grows. That is what fairies do. When you think of fairies you have to remember that they are as important as you are.

Have you seen a fairy? I know I have. For some reason fairies like dogs and they love to ride on their backs—most of the time up close to the dog person's ears—so they can hold on better, I suppose. But my friend Chipper sometimes has as many as ten fairies riding on his back—all at once. He has lots of room for them.

Here's a picture of Chipper. Do you see the fairies?

Fairies don't want to be disturbed when they are playing, so be careful and respectful when you walk in the woods. They love to play. Don't you?

When fairies play they are giving Mother Earth much joy. She loves their happiness. It is like a present for Mother Earth when fairies play. I would like to stress this point. Because your playing is a gift for Mother Earth too.

Playing should be thought of as a dance of joy. Even as the fairies play for Mother Earth, the games you play should be offerings of joy.

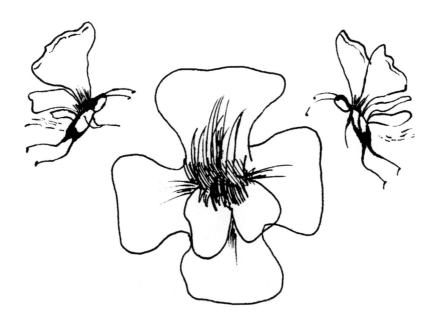

More Homework

The next time you decide to play, remember what I have said here. It's important. Games should be played for Mother Earth and all her family. So the next time you play, make your game a gift to the Earth. Take my advice.

I will talk more about Good Energy, the nature spirits and the angels, when we get together again. That will be LESSON THREE. Until then, I think that you have learned a lot. I know I have!

Delphi

Lesson Three
More About Angels

Angels want to work with you in partnership.

I know because I work with angels and they tell me.

Do you believe in angels? I do.

I wouldn't be surprised if I weren't an angel myself!

Delphi

The First Thing You Have to Know About Angels Is...

They change the pattern of energy in a room or anyplace where you are standing.

They make flashes of light where there weren't flashes before.

You can't miss the angels if you are really looking. And that's a fact.

I wouldn't want you to think that angels only come to small children or that only small children really believe in them. You see, angels are important for big people too.

As a matter of fact—if you can imagine this until you know the truth of it—the angels I am talking about are cosmic energies. That means that they are conscious and intelligent energy.

You don't have to think of angels with wings, you can think of them as complex energy forms. When they come into a room, for instance, they are like bosses of all the energies in the room. And they can make a place happy that has been sad. Invite an angel into your house and you will see.

If you say "hello" right away, the angel will stay with you. This is very important. Don't forget to say "hello" if you see an angel.

You can change the earth by first believing and then becoming a partner with Angel-Energy!

Can you remember this? Better write it down.

How to Be a Partner

Everybody has to learn about PARTNERSHIP.
You are all partners on this earth.
Spider and butterfly are partners
as are horse and bluebird.
We are all joined in a partnership.
We are a circle. Everyone's connected.
You see?

The balance of earth is maintained by partnership. That is the way we do things. You see, we all have to work together. It is when we fight that we get in trouble. If we could all be partners—and I mean EVERYONE—we wouldn't be arguing and hurting one another. There would be no wars EVER and there would always be good things to eat.

Remember your EARTH TREATY? Do you still have it with you? I'd like to have you look at it.

Think about this Treaty and what it means to you. Did you put anything about partnership in your Treaty? Could you please write something in your Treaty about partnership? I think it is important.

Angels Are Your Partners

I have to tell you a few things. Number one is that we really do have angels and nature spirits who help us. You can call them Good Energy. That's okay. Even if you can't see them the way we animals can, I want you to know that these people called angels are for real. They come in bunches of three mostly—but you can see a single angel sometimes, that is if you are trying hard enough. And sometimes they come in large amounts, maybe even thousands. I, myself, see angels all of the time. That's because I believe in them.

Maybe you don't believe in them anymore? Or maybe it is just that you have forgotten them. I'm here to remind you that angels do exist. And here's another thing. If you think that you are too big to think about angels, remember that's okay too. It's not what you call them that is important, it is who they are. Angels are Good Energy. Every time I say the name angel or nature spirit you can think GOOD ENERGY.

In the last lesson I told you about fairies. But there are other kinds of nature spirits or Good Energies who are part of the Angelic Kingdom. These nature spirits are not strangers to you. I think you have probably read about gnomes, haven't you?

Gnomes take care of your garden for you. They can be very stern but they mean well...these gnomes. They are the bosses of the nature spirits. If you are thinking that elves are the same as gnomes, they're not. Elves pester gnomes. But most of the nature spirits listen to the gnomes when they speak, just like most animals listen to me.

When you have a person who is a leader, you have a person who is going to be sure things are well taken care of. I think that is important, don't you? Would you like to be a leader?

I want to tell you a story about a gnome. Yes, gnomes are definitely energy, but SMART energy. I had a partner gnome who was a good friend of mine. His name was Geoffrey.

THIS IS GEOFFREY

Most gnomes don't take kindly to dogs like me eating all the vegetables in the garden. But there was this gnome who took care of the garden where I used to live in Virginia and he knew that I really liked carrots.

So every night this gnome invited me to come into the garden and he showed me the places where the biggest carrots were buried. Guess what? If we had a dry season and the ground was hard-packed, Geoffrey would ask his workers to loosen the soil where the carrots grew—just so I could have my carrot meal! No one knew about this but my gnome friend and me. We were the only ones! And we kept our secret very well.

And I want you to know something else.

I never forgot to say thank you, first to the Creator because He made the carrots, then to Geoffrey and his workers.

Always say THANK YOU. You will never want for a thing if you do this. You can see that I am very healthy and very happy, can't you?

Thank You

That's a big word, an important word,
and it opens many doors for you.

There is a secret about THANK YOU.
Thank you is the greatest power in
the universe.
Why is that, do you suppose?

What to Think About

Is Thank You an energy?

How can you make your life better by saying Thank You?

If you like magic, you'll find out thank you is powerful magic! Can you believe that?

Remember, Thank You is the greatest power in the universe!

HEY, THANK YOU!

What You Need to Know About the Nature Spirits

Now I have told you about gnomes, at least about Geoffrey. But there is more to say. Important words.

You have to understand that gnomes are really serious about their work. They like everything tidy, and they don't like people to pick flowers and fruit and twist branches off of trees without first ASKING.

You have to ask permission of all growing things before you cut, uproot or pick them.

Listen!

Don't pick anything without permission. And never cut down a tree—not even for Christmas—without first asking the tree itself if it is okay. Sometimes trees want to stay where they are and don't want to be cut.

And here is something else you should know...Guess who might be standing beside the tree when you are thinking about twisting a branch or cutting it down? A gnome! And I have to tell you, you will have a friend for life if you ask permission.

If people could learn that we are all partners and we can live together without hurting one another, that would make Mother Earth very happy.

Would you like to see a gnome helping our friends the trees? I thought that you would; just turn this page.

Your Friend the Gnome

Most people can't see gnomes but everyone can FEEL them. It is a wonderful feeling when you have a gnome with you. As a team, you can't be beat. You remember I said to you it was okay to call a gnome SMART ENERGY? You could even call him SMART for short.

And it is the same with all the other nature spirits. They are all smart energies that can help you in your garden, in the air that you breathe, in the water that you drink, and in keeping your fires under control.

While we are on the subject of fires, I have to tell you here and now that those nature spirits who are responsible for fire do not like anyone playing with matches. If you want to be a friend of the nature spirits, SMART ENERGY, then do not start a fire unless it is perfectly safe to do so. If you are a child, and reading what I have to say here, just don't light matches at all. Okay? Respect fire. It can really be a problem if you don't!

Meet Some of the Smart Energies

There is the wind sprite or SYLPH who is trying to help us have clean air.

There is the UNDINE who wants us to take care of our oceans and all our lakes and streams.

There is the SALAMANDER who asks us to please respect fire and to say thank you for the warmth we receive from it.

And don't forget the GNOME who helps earth and keeps her green.

They all work together to make our planet a happier place to live.

Indeed, all these little people work very hard for us, but we need to know that they EXIST and that they are our PARTNERS in the environment.

I am certain you know that our Earth is really having a hard time—what with pollution and too many trees being chopped down! We have to take care of her and be partners with her just like I told you before.

And when we know that there are angels and nature spirits—Good Energies—ready to help us, then we can work together to make Mother Earth clean and pure and safe for all of us—all creatures great and small.

I think that this is an important part of my lesson for you to think about.

Here Is Some Homework

Decide now to work with Good Energy.

Be partners with the angel community. They will help you to think of projects that you can organize—remember what I said about a leader?

And here is the secret. When you believe in the Good Energies—you know who I am talking about—and you partner with them, they will help you to make a better planet, a safer planet and a happier planet. This would probably get you the Nobel Peace Prize. I'll bet!

Delphi

Lesson Four
All About Listening

Open your ears and your heart.
If you can't listen this way,
you won't hear a thing.

Delphi

Taking Time to Listen

I am going to try to explain to you the importance of listening. This is something you haven't gotten straight on this planet. People talk too much. Perhaps you have noticed this. I know I have.

When you are talking you aren't listening. Everything is learned by listening and no one learns anything by talking. Have you noticed that? I know I have.

In the next few hours while you are taking my lesson to heart, I want you to really think about the power of LISTENING. Because—as I have told you before—listening will give you knowledge and wisdom. I have more to say about this.

When you are ready to LISTEN you are ready to learn. And that LEARNING part is very important. As you grow and learn more about the secret things we can tell you about the earth, you will have the attention of everyone around you. Even the flies and the birds will stop to hear you talk.

But the best thing I have to tell you on this page is listen not only with your ears but with your heart. And when you do this, you will hear all of us in the animal world, and you will have the song of our hearts in your heart too. You will have friends all over the earth when you listen with your heart and you will never be alone. Not ever!

Come on—I'll show you more—just read on.

Delphi

Listening Is Power

The power of listening must be taught in schools so you can grow. How do you ever expect to grow if you don't listen? That is very important. Listening and growing go together.

I can't imagine not listening first before I speak. Then there is ALWAYS AN ANSWER. Because answers come from listening.

"Why don't you listen?" I have to ask myself again and again. It puzzles me. Honestly, it does. I am going to teach you to listen as you read these pages. Have a seat beside me. I know you can't see me but IMAGINE I am with you. Okay? Here is my picture so you can remember what I look like.

Now let's talk about listening and why it is so important in your life.

When you listen to people you can hear what they are really saying. They are not always saying what you think they are saying, so you had better listen with your heart and your ears the way I do.

If people would stop to listen to each other, there would be more UNDERSTANDING on earth. We could use a little more of that, don't you think?

The first thing for you to know about listening is that you are respectful of a person when you listen—and that person will respect you back.

This RULE
applies to all of life,
even the little crickets!

What can you tell me about a cricket's song? Go ahead. Try! Make a sound like a cricket if you can. Now if you can't, it just means you haven't listened. So get busy and LISTEN to the cricket with your ears and your heart and just maybe that cricket will say more than just his tuneful song. I mean...these crickets have a lot of information—good information—important information—for you and for me. We have to listen. And if you don't have a cricket where you live, then you can pick another partner. But LISTEN!

Hear me out on this one, there is more. Listen to the way you walk on this earth. I am really serious about this. Because you want to be a part of the whole community of nature. Take, for instance, a jungle. How would you walk in a jungle? Please write in your notebook what you think about this.

I'll tell you one more thing about the jungle. There isn't one animal or bird or snake or plant that won't appreciate the way you walk in harmony with their environment.

Questions

1. What does the word HARMONY mean? Write what you think harmony means.

2. Why is it important to walk in harmony with all your sisters and brothers on the planet?

Practice This

IMAGINE that you ARE walking in peace and in harmony with your fellow creatures, with everyone you know and all the people of the earth. I know, it seems impossible, but IMAGINE. Just pretend for a moment the way you pretended to sit beside me.

Sometimes, when I imagine, I create pictures in my mind and heart. Like today, talking to you this way, I am imagining a picture of people all around the earth holding hands. And they are very happy. You can see it in their faces. They are all wearing great big smiles.

And guess what?

They are singing the cricket song!

Try this idea. Because every time you imagine a picture, like the one I just gave you, you will find someone else who thinks the same way.

You know about the internet, don't you? Hey, you may even have your own web site or have your name linked with someone who does. Maybe you could begin a pink ribbon circle around the earth—and see people holding hands and liking each other!

Or...

Maybe we could start this idea together on my web site. You have that address, don't you? If you don't, here it is: www.delphinet.org. You can e-mail me about this idea at delphinet@mindspring.com! Let's be partners!

Back to Listening

I am ready to tell you more about listening. Most important is that you know that everyone speaks.

Everybody is talking. Not everyone understands this but it is true. The mountain lion talks and the mouse talks. They are all speaking! Each one has an important message and they all say things to each other—even though maybe you cannot hear them.

Remember when I asked you to listen with both your ears and your heart? We can all communicate better when we do this. The reason people have wars is because they have not been communicating the right way. You know what I said—through the ears and the heart! So let's learn communication the correct way, shall we? THE DELPHI WAY!

Important Points to Remember

THE FIRST THING you have to do is **BE QUIET**. Someone has something to say. How are you going to hear that person (could be a mouse, you know!) if you are busy talking? Listening is powerful. I tell you that right now.

THE SECOND THING is **RESPECT**. That's when you are humble enough and quiet enough to know that every person—could be four-legged, could be two-legged—might even be a bird in the air or a worm on the ground—deserves your respect.

We are all important and we are all citizens of Mother Earth!

That business of one person being more important than another has got to stop. There is no species more important than another. We are all loved the same by our Creator. Keep that in mind. That is what will stop the wars and keep our planet healthy and happy.

THE THIRD THING I want to talk to you about is **LOVE**. When you want to understand what another person is saying or when you want them to understand you, the best way is through the heart. Be loving.

When you love someone—despite the differences you might have—you make a friend of that person.

Everybody needs love. We all do. And if you love with your heart the way I do, you'll have friends all over the earth. You will be able to understand them when they speak. World peace is made this way.

Think about loving
more than you think
about yourself.
I have more secrets like
this. KEEP READING!

More Thoughts About Listening

Birds have a way of talking. They are very friendly and polite—most of them. Take time off and watch the birds as they communicate. You can almost tell what they are saying by sitting still and watching them talk together.

The next time you take a walk, listen. Stop and hear the leaves and the river. Listen to the wind—and the coyote's howl. What's he saying? Hear the Creator speaking in your heart and hear the mooing of the cows. I love cows, don't you? They are so peaceful.

A horse's whinny has lots of information. Trees speak. There is so much you can learn when you LISTEN.

You will find peace in your heart when you LISTEN.

I want to thank you for listening.

Delphi

Lesson Five
Practicing Being Good

What matters most is your heart.
And how you care about people and animals.
Loving your animal friends is very important.
No one loves enough on this planet.
I think you can do better than you are doing.

Delphi

Superdogs

Dogs are very important teachers. They can tell you about yourself faster than anybody.

Lots of times a dog will sniff first before saying "hello." Have you noticed that? They can tell by sniffing your hand or any part of you what kind of person you are. If you are truthful, they will know. They can smell truthfulness.

Always let a dog sniff your hand and your clothing. That's being polite. Dogs like to know who they are talking to before they begin. You can't fool a dog, you know. You might be able to fool people but not a dog. They know who you are right away, and how much you can be trusted as a friend!

The time has come for people to understand dogs better. We are not stupid, you know. Far from it! And we can be your best friend when we trust each other.

I want to trust you right now. Is that okay? I hope you trust me. There are things that you haven't told anyone, but you can trust me to listen. And I won't judge you for anything you may have done because I love you. And love doesn't judge.

Can you love me back?
I am your friend.

Delphi

Living Truthfully

The first person you have to be truthful with is yourself. If you can face yourself in the mirror and say "I love you" to yourself and really mean it, you are well on your way to being a good person.

Next time you look in the mirror, say "I love you" and really mean it. When you can do this, you will have a happy heart.

But what about all the people who don't feel good about themselves? This is where you come in. You can make them feel better about themselves by smiling at them. And if that doesn't work—try giving them a present. Even a kind word can change the way they think about themselves. That's a fact!

Try doing one good deed a day.

You have a notebook, don't you? Well, okay. Here's what I want you to do—it will help the planet, you know—keep track of all your good deeds day by day. Write them all in your notebook so that you can go back over them and feel good about yourself.

A GOOD DEED always comes from a KIND HEART. That is really where it all starts, the kind heart. If you want to help people, they will feel it in their hearts. Then they will smile. Happiness is a good thing to have on the earth. If you can help people be happy, that would be a real, solid contribution.

So my plan for today is to wish you a happy heart and then to ask you to record your good deeds—at least one per day minimum. I wouldn't ask you to do this unless it was important.

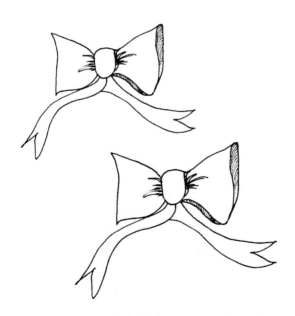

That is what my Pink Ribbon Club is all about. It is about people feeling good about themselves and other people and dogs, too. It's about LOVE.

You can't stop once you start making people feel happy. You will really find out that it is FUN to make people smile and FUN to pay extra special attention to someone!

I don't mean to repeat myself, but it is important. The color pink really means love. It is a color that can make people feel happy and appreciated. I would like you to color this ribbon pink.

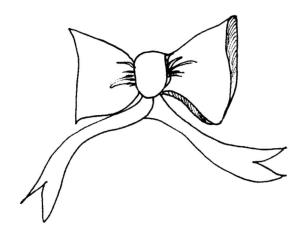

If you would like to join my club, your pink ribbon makes you a member. That means that you and I are PARTNERS

and...

can make a difference
on earth
by our good deeds
and kind hearts.

I have lots of other things I want to talk to you about, and lots of ways we can work together as a TEAM to make Mother Earth a happy place to live.

Here's your HOMEWORK. This week, do a good deed from your kind heart every day and record it in your notebook. And remember to smile. You will see a lot of changes in your own life when you do this!

Animals Have Hearts Too

I wouldn't tell you this if it were not true. It is very important to realize that we are all part of the Circle of Life. Our contributions as animals are just as important as yours. This hasn't been understood very well on earth. I know you can help people to understand.

Helpful Questions

What contribution to the Circle of Life does the cow make?

What contribution to the Circle of Life does the lion make?

What contribution does the dog make?

What contribution do you make?

It is not enough just to have a "pet" at home. That is not enough! Every animal on this planet loves you. Perhaps you can't believe this yet, but it is true.

Won't it be a wonderful planet when we all remember how much we are loved?

I love you,

Delphi

Practice This

When you see an animal, ask that animal partner to be your friend. When you do that you build a FRIENDSHIP CIRCLE. That circle will be with you everywhere you go, even in your dreams. I can't imagine you ever having a nightmare with all of us watching over you!

All animals are your friends and love you, even if you don't know it yet. Because you respect all animals and call them your friends, you will not want to bother them. Lions and tigers have their own lives to live. They can be your friends and not live in the same house with you. Get my point? Respect all animals, but don't get too close to them unless they want you to!

It's the same with dogs. Respect the dogs you meet and they will respect you. If you pull their ears or tails, you are not showing respect and you may lose their friendship right away. Besides, you hurt us when you pull on our body parts.

To be a friend is to be kind,
considerate and always thoughtful
of our well-being.
Kind deeds are for animals too.

Don't forget us! Would you please include us when you are writing in your notebook about good deeds? Do a kind deed for us at least two times a week. Thanks a lot!

Do you need a few examples of how you can help the animal kingdom with your good deeds? I have a few good ideas for you.

Delphi's Suggestions

1. If you have animal friends who live with you, be sure that they always have a full bowl of fresh water. They should never be without water. That is very important.

2. If you are walking by a horse who looks lonely or who wants to visit with you, please stop and say "hello." Horses love company and they love to communicate.

3. If you notice a dog or cat who doesn't have a collar or who looks lost and hungry, tell someone or call an animal rescue shelter right away. We all have to help each other when we are in trouble.

Well, those are a few ideas of kind deeds, but you will think of lots more.

Last Thoughts of the Day

I have to tell you that a KIND HEART is the most important quality you can have.

When you smile, always begin your smile from your KIND HEART. Then it will be a real smile and all of nature will smile with you!

Your kind deeds must begin from your heart. Then they are sincere kind deeds and are meaningful to everyone.

Create a game out of being kind and making people and animals happy. It goes like this...

PLEASE
TURN
THIS
PAGE...

You just smile
and do something nice for someone
and watch how they change.

Then, keep notes about this in your notebook.

Keep a record of how you have
caused changes in people's lives.

Maybe they were sad or lonely
or even sour
before you helped them out
by your kind heart.

Why don't you buy a balloon so that at the end of these lessons you can blow it up? See if you can find a SMILE BALLOON.

A smile balloon will help you to always remember how you can make a big difference in hundreds—maybe thousands—of people's lives, animals too. It's by SMILING and doing GOOD DEEDS.

Hey! You know what? Your smile can change the world!

So, thanks for being on earth with me.

Your friend,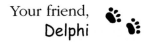
Delphi

Lesson Six
Living Peacefully

Hi! My name is Delphi and we have met before.
Now I would like to talk about Rats and Cats.

Rats and Cats

When you think people don't get along, they almost never do. Take, for instance, Rats and Cats. You probably have an idea that they don't like each other very much. What if I told you that they actually work together in partnership on our planet?

We all are partners in the animal kingdom. As a matter of fact everyone, including me, is agreed that we are partners. Well...almost everyone. You see, we have a problem with some people because they are not partners yet. Maybe a few are...but not too many.

When the Creator made this earth and all the creatures and the plants, He was very specific about balance. He said that we all would be happy and well-fed if we remembered to help each other and help our Mother Earth. That's what partnership means—HELPING ONE ANOTHER.

What happened when the Creator told us to be partners is a long story. I think it is probably too long to tell right now. The most important part is that human beings became so busy with their own affairs that they separated themselves from us. They broke the chain of partnership. They forgot to feel partnership with all life! And that's when the trouble began.

That's not to say that we can't make things better— you and I—we can! And we will! If you will be my partner, I will introduce you to other partners, so we can work together as a team and move mountains, so to speak.

Delphi

Believing It Is So

Who would believe nowadays that Rats and Cats are partners? That's not an acceptable belief, is it?

There are other beliefs like: lambs don't like lions—chickens don't like coyotes—people don't like sharks. Why, you have countries that don't like other countries. Religions that don't like other religions. It just goes on and on. It is like that when you forget the Creator's words—that we are all partners on earth.

If you can believe in what I am telling you, you will change your whole way of thinking. In fact, it is my belief that you can change the world!

It is when we are helping each other and the earth that we are partners. Take me, for instance. I was invited to an event called *The Gathering*. This is an event where many different types of what you might call "wild animals"—who are also movie stars—gather to say "hello" to the public. And I was invited! It was quite an honor because no other dog was asked to be present.

So—when I received my invitation to attend, my partner Pat was worried. She didn't think I would get along with "wild animal" movie stars—like lions, tigers and elephants. She had the Rats and Cats frame of mind.

Well, we all got along just fine.

We were partners, you see, on the same assignment—to introduce people to our WORLD OF PARTNERSHIP.

Once, when Pat saw how nicely I got along with a cougar, I told her that it was because we were all at *The Gathering* to HELP. You see, that is what the Creator had in mind when He said we were to be partners.

Rats and Cats! You see?

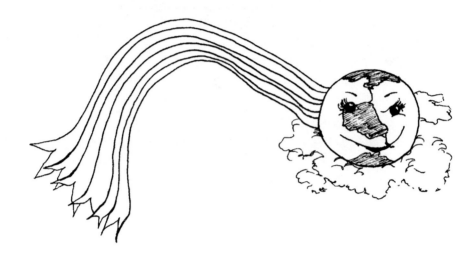

My Important Philosophy
by Delphi

Often people fight wars or argue or are afraid of each other because they believe that they are different. They think they are special or not special—whatever the case may be. But the REAL truth is we are all equal. That is what true partnership is all about. I have to tell you that this is the way to world peace. I couldn't be more right on this point.

If you would look at everyone you meet as a genuine partner, I think you would find you have more friends than ever before! Your increase in friends would be substantial and you would be helping the earth by being friends with everyone.

Mother Earth wants everyone to be friendly.

There is no reason why you can't be friendly,
she says.

Unfriendliness is a bad habit that people
have learned and now have to forget.

You don't have to stay in a bad habit,
you know.

Habits can be forgotten!

What Mother Earth really needs is a partnership of people and animals.

Pretend you are at *The Gathering* right now. You can sit with a lion at *The Gathering*—that is, if you are invited and the trainer is close by. Imagine you are sitting with a lion at *The Gathering* and everybody is watching—tiger, elephant, kangaroo, monkey. They send you good thoughts while you are sitting there with the lion. And everybody is happy.

If you think about this, you will be much happier in your life. You can't be lonely or afraid because you have friends everywhere—REAL FRIENDS! They are your partners for life. No one is supposed to be lonely or afraid.

Everywhere you go
you will have a special
friend like squirrel, rabbit,
horse, bird.
Oh, I could go on and on.
Because friends are
everywhere!

But the best part of this is—Mother Earth knows you love her and that you respect her. She can feel you picking up litter and helping to keep her streets and rivers clean. She can actually FEEL you walking softly on her with all your friends. This makes her happy and she smiles.

I want you to remember that when people argue and say mean things about one another, it hurts Mother Earth. Everyone needs to be kind to one another. The environment would improve one hundred percent.

If we could all be happy together it would really help Mother Earth. Let's try it, okay?

A Pleasant Place to Be

You know what a rainbow looks like, don't you?

Many colors joined together is a beautiful sight. You will agree with that, I know. The partnership I have been speaking about is a lot like the rainbow. Do you know why?

Remember when I was at *The Gathering* and we all worked together there—tiger and lion and monkey and your friend Delphi? And when I said that we all got along because we were all there to help—well, that's the rainbow, isn't it?

Here's a thought. If we all lived together on earth in a rainbow, wouldn't there be peace on earth and wouldn't we all be happy?

Think about the rainbow for a minute. What does the rainbow tell you about peace?

Here Is What I Think

What if the lion was red, the rat was yellow, the cat was green, the spider was blue and you were the purple color in the rainbow? Do you see how all the different colors fit together to make one beautiful rainbow?

Well, let me tell you something...Life is like that— your life and mine. We can fit together and be a rainbow! This is partnership; this is RATS AND CATS!

This is a rainbow.

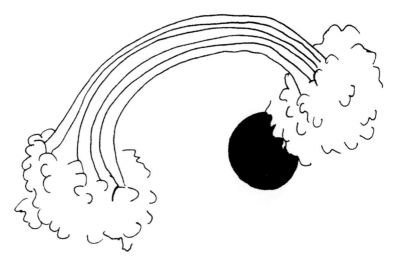

Who is your red partner? Your yellow partner? Your green partner and blue partner? Think of partners that you wouldn't normally put together—like Rats and Cats. Don't forget to add your name. You are part of the rainbow, you know!

Last Minute Instructions

We have talked about a lot of things. How you can be happy and how you can make others happy. We have even talked about how dogs can speak.

This will be fun! Open to the first page of LESSON ONE. That is the page where I start talking about myself—Delphi.

Make a list of everything important that I have taught you. You can take all the time you want because I have said a lot and I want you to remember everything!

More to Do

Cut a strip of paper. The heavy kind is best. What would you like to remember more than anything else from these lessons? Write that down on your DELPHI BOOKMARK.

That bookmark will go everywhere with you. Take it to school or put it in your favorite book. You will remember me, all right, with that bookmark!

I hope you have had a good time with me. I have had a good time with you. Keep smiling! You can make a difference. Remember, we are all here to help.

I'll be seeing you,

Delphi

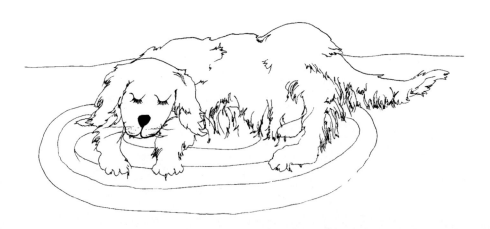

Delphi's Song

It's a whole new world! It's a world that's made for you and for me. Come

jump in - to the cir-cle now. — My name is Del -phi. It's a whole new world! It's a

world where there's a lot to see, why don't you come and join with me? My name is Del - phi.

Acknowledgements

You know who you are!
Thank you for being my partner!

Delphi

Here Are Ways to Help

Many groups around the world care for the Circle of Life. If you would like to learn about some of these groups and about how you can be of help, you can contact:

Center for International Cooperation
(www.cicngo.org)
e-mail: cic@cicngo.org
phone: 805-640-6430
P.O. Box 913, Ojai, California 93024
(Sponsor of Delphi's web site, www.delphinet.org, which has links to many organizations that help animals and our planet.)

Children of the Earth United
(www.childrenoftheearth.org)
e-mail: entry@childrenoftheearth.org
phone: 301-371-0764
P.O. Box 271, Middletown, Maryland 21769

Defenders of Wildlife
(www.defenders.org)
e-mail: info@defenders.org
phone: 202-682-9400
1101 14th Street, NW #1400
Washington, D.C. 20005

Humane Society of the United States
(www.hsus.org)
phone: 202-452-1100
2100 L Street NW
Washington, D.C. 20037

International Wildlife Coalition
(www.iwc.org)
e-mail: iwchq@iwc.org
phone: 508-548-8328
70 East Falmouth Highway
East Falmouth, Massachusetts 02536

Kids4Earth
(www.kids4earth.org)
e-mail: info@kids4earth.org. phone: 805-646-2473
P.O. Box 1440
Ojai, California 93024

**National Association for Humane
and Environmental Education**
(www.nahee.org)
e-mail: nahee@nahee.org. phone: 860-434-8666
P.O. Box 362
East Haddam, Connecticut 06423-0362

National Humane Education Society
(www.nhes.org)
e-mail: nhesinformation@nhes.org
phone: 304-725-0506
P.O. Box 340
Charles Town, West Virginia 25414-0340

Positive Futures Network

(www.futurenet.org)
e-mail: yes@futurenet.org
phone: 800-937-4451
P.O. Box 10818
Bainbridge Island, Washington 98110-0818

United Nations CyberSchoolBus

(www.un.org/Pubs/CyberSchoolBus)
e-mail: cyberschoolbus@un.org
phone: 212-963-8589
United Nations
Global Teaching and Learning Project
c/o Cyberschoolbus
One UN Plaza
Room DC1-552
New York, New York 10017

Wildlife Awareness Foundation

(www.wildlifeaware.org)
e-mail: info@wildlifeaware.org
phone: 949-721-0204
537 Newport Center Drive #588
Newport Beach, California 92660

World Animal Net (www.worldanimal.net)

e-mail: info@worldanimal.net
phone: 617-524-3670
19 Chestnut Square
Boston, Massachusetts 02130
and 420 Bronco Road
Soquel, California 95073

World Wildlife Fund
(www.wwf.org)
phone: 800-CALL-WWF
1250 Twenty-fourth Street, NW
P.O. Box 97180
Washington, D.C. 20090-7180

Yes! Action Camps
Youth for Environmental Sanity
(www.yesworld.org)
e-mail: camps@yesworld.org
phone: 877-293-7226
420 Bronco Road
Soquel, California   95073

About the Authors

Patricia Jepsen

From early childhood Patricia Jepsen was surrounded with the love of animals and considered all animals her friends. The gift of interspecies communication developed as her consciousness evolved to embrace all life as sacred.

For over twenty-five years, Ms. Jepsen has been active in the expanding spiritual and environmental movements as a writer, lecturer and seminar leader. She is the founder and director of the Center for International Cooperation (CIC), a non-governmental organization that is affiliated with the United Nations. In 1989, CIC cosponsored one of the first global conferences to present indigenous wisdom as an earth-saving message. Currently, CIC is sponsoring an educational program that focuses on partnership with all life and communication with animals. This project is a result of the teachings realized in "Communication with Animals" classes that Ms. Jepsen held with Delphi, her eldest golden retriever, from 1997 to 1999.

Ms. Jepsen is a highly experienced presenter. She has been a professional actor and teacher in the field of creative arts. She travels globally, speaking, holding seminars and workshops, and convening conferences. *Six Lessons with Delphi, How to Live Happily with All Life* serves as an educational pilot program in Tucson, Arizona, through restorative justice and supplementary character-building programs within schools and community-based youth groups.

Delphi has a web site: www.delphinet.org, a newsletter, *DelphiNews,* and a Delphi Club that enlists children and adults to help animals and the environment.

Delphi

Delphi came to Pat Jepsen from a fine kennel in Virginia. She had been a show dog but was not happy about that profession. It must have been ordained, Delphi often thinks, because when she met Pat she knew she had found her spokesperson.

Since that time, Delphi has co-authored with Pat *Delphi, What Being on Earth Is All About,* written *Six Lessons with Delphi,* and has taught many workshops and classes. She is in the process of forming a school based on her teachings in *Six Lessons.* This course has received funding from the City of Tucson's Graffiti Abatement Program and is under consideration as a restorative justice program in Pima County, Arizona.

Delphi's expectations are high. She wishes to reach the world with her vision of the circle of life. And, she confides, "I hope to seat myself at the United Nations where I can speak to everybody about partnership and a new earth!" You can learn more about Delphi and her network by visiting her web site: www.delphinet.org.